The Trojan Horse

By

Erich J Goller

Published

by

Passion for Poetry Publishers

Cover art work and all interior pictures,
By
Pat Simpson.

©2008 by Erich J Goller
All rights reserved. No part of this book may be reproduced, stored in a retrieval system or transmitted in any form by any means without the prior permission of the publishers, except by a reviewer who may quote brief passages in a review to be printed in a newspaper, magazine or journal.
ISBN   978-0-6151-9266-6

Contents Page One

1	The Trojan Horse
2	Why? Why?
3	Peace in the world
4	When Words Begin To fail
5	Hello America
6	A New Beginning
7	American Eagle
8	The First Step
9	Serene Hours
10	Another World
11	Faith and Trust
12	Open Door
13	The Universe
14	A World without Trees
15	far Away
16	Narrow Streets
17	Silent Nature
18	Forever There
19	A Time for Change
20	Mother Nature
21	Alpine Meadow
22	Positive Attitude
23	Color's (#1)
24	The Master's Touch
25	Tick-Tock
26	The Shield in My Life
27	Greener Grass
28	Blackout
29	Equal Time
30	My Daily bread
31	True Reflection
32	Schatzi
33	My Little Girl
34	Gone To Heaven
35	Retired
36	I Miss You
37	The Senior Years
38	I've Learned

Contents Page Two

39	I am Safely Home My Dear
40	Letters
41	A True Fan
42	The Siren
43	The Worlds Best Medicine
44	Junk Mail
45	White Horse
46	The Moon Tears Legend
47	Mysterious Seven Seas
48	Growing Up
49	If Cars Could Talk
50	Always
51	Dreamer
52	Color Your Life
53	My Soft feathered Friends
54	Our Grandparents
55	My Favorite Season
56	Mysterious Sky
57	Morning Pleasures
58	The Fire Salamander Train
59	A Winters Portrait
60	My Inspirations
61	Life's Gift
62	Another Year Older
63	Strolling on the Beach
64	Fresh Fallen Snow
65	Computers
66	The Hills Are Alive
67	Limitations
68	Treasured Time
69	Treasured Time
70	The Last Goodbye
71	Love and Joy
72	That's Amore
73	Noel
74	Well Winter
75	A Heavenly Dream
76	A Sunny Christmas

Contents Page Three

77	Baked Rabbit
78	Love from A to Z
79	Misguided Dreams
80	A Magical Season
81	Embracing Life
82	Grand Canyon
83	Coonhound
84	Life as A Tree
85	Seeking for Answers
86	Let all the Church Bells Ring
87	Life's Light
88	Rhapsodies
89	The Brown Shirts
90	The Brown Shirts
91	I Love Them all
92	Footsteps
93	Three wishes
94	Love is Like
95	The Beetle
96	A Light From Beyond
97	Big Bang
98	All Within
99	Transition
100	Dream Paradise
101	No Internet in Heaven
102	My Favorite Place
103	Guiding Light & Scarlet Sky
104	Inner Vision
105	Christmas In Heaven
106	Precious Things
107	My Birthday Wish
108	Things of Joy and Beauty
109	Aimless
110	Splendor Moments
111	To Be Or Not
112	Edelweiss. & Far Beyond
113	Colors #2
114	My Photo Album
115	Flashbacks
116	Window of Tomorrow

Foreword

Erich was born in Vienna, raised as a Catholic.
He has three brothers and one sister.
He lost his parents before he was aged 40.
A world war two survivors!
In the mid fifties the family moved to California,
51 years ago Erich married his school sweetheart,
And they raised two children, a boy and a girl.
In Los Angeles he made his living as a mechanic and partly
As an Actor in TV and motion pictures,
"under the name of Eric Forst"
Eight years ago after living 44 years in Los Angels he moved to Nashville
To be with his daughter and grandchildren!
He started writing poetry about ten years ago; some of his poems have been published By Noble House,
The International Library of Poetry, Famous Poets Society, League of American Poets, Poets World Wide and others....
This collection of poetry has been written from true-life experience,
growing up, travel, nature, happy times,
Romantic, faith, humor, loss, dreams, and fantasy!
The Title for this book and poem
"The Trojan Horse"
Was inspired from that tragic September 11th.
He is now living in Nashville where he resides with his
Family and continues writing poetry, acting and some
Amateur painting! Erich's poetry is written for
All ages to enjoy, and he hopes it will take you on
A Pleasant Journey!

Dedication

To my wife Mimi and my family And
All my friends who encouraged
Me to continue writing!

A special thanks to the publishers
Patricia Ann Farnsworth-Simpson and
Daveda Gruber for their direction in
Preparing my manuscript
For publication!

God Bless America!

The two aeroplanes flew in,

Like the Trojan Horse with a friendly grin,

"But inside the plane, some men did linger there

To do harm without care!

&****&

The Trojan Horse

America the beautiful
And not so long ago the free,
A Trojan horse they built
That no-one else could see.

Out they did creep, one by one!
To do us harm
As much as can be done,
With all the fear and sorry
That they have done,
Terrorists will not bring America down.

United as never before
They have brought the fight back
To their own door!
Never must they be able to
Build a Trojan horse again.

Freedom will take the course
Back to where it used to be,
To America the beautiful
America and the free.

&****&

Why? Why?

On that sunny September day
There was utter confusion
Suddenly the twin towers
After immense fiery explosions,
Were crashing to the ground,
For many, time had run out.

A horrifying sight of destruction,
Burning and frightful screaming,
Senseless death and endless tears,
Why?
For America to be confronted
With the worst fears.

After this longest September 11th day
Life will never be the same
Just as long as our America
Remains fair game.

United we shall and must stand
Freedom will always be an American trend,
To hopefully bring all that terror
Forever to an end.
Then we might never have to ask
WHY?

&****&

Peace in the World

Through the ages now and before
Men have always been at war.
Though storms will rage around us
And many things may go wrong,
For everything there is a reason
But there is no excuse for war,
Not Anymore.

There was a time when one could
Travel without fear,
When things in this world were fair
People seemed to care.
The nations are in agreement
When trading their goods,
Why can't they trade their wisdom
For Peace.

Now dark clouds of war loom above,
Let everyone in this world
Take the time and pause
To exhale all the hate
Let the spirit of the Lord
Flow between them all, and then
Their shall be peace in the world
For Evermore.

There should be no more excuses to start a war.

&****&

When Words Begin To Fail

When words and the nature
Of humanity begin to fail,
How did the human beings
Come to be what they are?
And for what are we in this world.

When words begin to fail
We need to remember and understand
The Lord made this earth
And all this beautiful land
For every color and creed
To tend and live in peace.

When words begin to fail
We can cry with those in mourning
Give them hope anew,
But without peace
Our planet is doomed.

When words begin to fail
And no hope is in sight,
Look towards heaven
The light of God shines ever bright.

When words begin to fail
Just raise two fingers for the symbol of peace
Instead of putting them on triggers,
For we must make all wars cease.

When words begin to fail
That's no reason for war or heartache,
Let's plow the fields, plant the seeds,
With food for all and no hunger tears,
So we live in peace, without these fears.

&****&

Hello America

Bring sunshine, laughter and happiness
Back into your heart,
Hate and anger will not change,
War and destruction longing to exhale.

Don't let the dark clouds dismay you
Don't waste another day.
Always remember the past
And that tragic September day.

Focus on the light ahead
as you go along your way.
Control will conquer the fear;
As you confront each given precious day
For as long as you are here.

No one knows what lies ahead,
There will be many trials to bear
God knows not everything is fair.

Peace and wisdom must prevail
Then freedom shall have its way,
Because America is here to stay.

&****&

A New Beginning

From around the world they come
To Uncle Sam's welcoming arms,
To have an opportunity
For a better life to be,
A chance to work
To raise a family.

Where they can talk and walk,
Live as they please,
Practice their religion
Whatever it might be.

One day become an
American citizen,
To live within the land
Of the proud and the free,
Where everyone can cherish
True liberty.

America the best place to live.

&****&

American Eagle

Springing from a rift in the rock
A sapling of a mountain pine!
An eagle perched high
Upon a mountain crag,
Nesting with his eaglets and mate.

Fearless in spirit;
Conscious of their power,
With the wings outstretched
Flying in the breeze
Like a glider,
Looking for prey
To nourish the young.

Soaring Mountain high,
Magnificent,
The spirit of liberty,
The American eagle.

Let's assure their survival

&****&

The First Step

The first step is often the hardest
That everyone has to take.
We often become discouraged
When we fall down,
These obstacles have to be overcome.

Excited or frightened
It all begins with the first step,
Learning to walk, run, or to dance;
The first day of school or a romance.

Some dreams may fuel a fire
May reach that goal to show,
But if we don't take that first step
We will never know.

Not every first step gives you the vision
To make the right decision!
That path that seems so right
Is for everyone to know,
Like each has his private rainbow.

Never be afraid to take that first step
Try to do your best,
If you have faith
The Lord will help you with the rest.

&*****&

Serene Hours

A time when I find peace
In things I understand
To bring back joyful memories
So I forget things that bother me.

A time to behold the great blue sky,
The beauty of the rising sun
To embrace and kiss my love
Feel his blessings from above.

A time to spend with family and friends,
With books I long to read
Hours of comfort with peace reflective,
To keep a long-range perspective.

A time to know your heart
And show you mine,
Let my lips speak only of love each day
To see my life in a different way.

A time when the pillow meets my head
My thoughts are fading to their sleep
The moon shines on high so bright
Like a dream that is waiting for the night.

&****&

Another World

Frowned on by society!
Stripped of human dignity!
Always terrified, hungry,
Cold and in pain,
A terrible feeling of going insane.

Searching the trash for something to eat,
For old newspaper and cardboard
To keep me warm at night
Anywhere I can find a place to sleep.

Longing for something warm to eat or drink,
What is the answer for a sufferer in need?
I am so afraid of the dark
And every night I pray
Please dear God take me away
Relieve me from my pain.

I have no hope for tomorrow,
Just wandering aimlessly,
Homeless!
A life not worth living.

It is so very sad that some humans,
Have to live like animals on the street,
In wealthy country's where billions
Are being wasted on senseless wars.

&****&

Faith and Trust

Living in a "New Age"
Under one universal sky
That we all must share,
And to live in peace
Everyone in the world must care.

We live in a dangerous time indeed,
It's not just our highways or in the air
But throughout the world everywhere,
If there will be wars rather than peace
Many hearts will forever weep and grieve.

Many religious beliefs
Being celebrated around the world
Indeed every person is different,
No two people are the same
But all have to walk through the same GATE

If all would honor the differences
Learn to accept each other
Then God will shine a guiding light
For all mankind to see
The road leading to a peaceful destiny.

Open Door

Everybody in this world
Has their own unique way of seeing and feeling things.
He cannot solve all problems but to those who believe
He will offer cheer to ease their pain.

Everyone wishes for earthly things,
For wealth, love and joy which; only pleasure brings,
For all the simple things in life
That gives our heart delight.

We each have our private rainbow if we just look and see.
In spite of what we know is right
It is hard to walk alone
Through life, when we are tired and worn.

It is His love and strength which brings salvation,
His door is always open wide
For everyone is welcome inside.
Yes! His door is always open, no reservation is needed.

&****&

The Universe

Could intelligent life evolve twice?
More advanced than our own?
Are we alone?

To far beyond to compare in this world
As distinguished from Heaven and Hell!
Flaming mountains against the blue sky
And winds that howls and moan,
Are we alone?

Though hidden from our view
What must we assume?
A wild creation,
A possible duplication
Where every man may roam?
Are we alone?

All that expands from the sky
Makes one stop and wonder,
Is there life beyond our nature?
Yet no one knows
This Universe of tomorrow,
Are we alone?

In motion pictures life exists beyond our planet

&****&

A World Without Trees

The thought really scares me,
How bare everything would be
If our heavenly Father
Hadn't planted all the trees.

What would be the story
With Adam and Eve?
They wouldn't have had clothes
If there were no leaves.

Where would the apes have lived?
Or the birds made their nests?
Noah could not have built the ark
To save his family and animals from the flood.

There would be no wood to make a fire;
All the nights would be very cold and dark.
Would there be life as we know today?
There would be no fruit to eat, no Christmas trees.

No seafaring ships to sail the seven seas.
All the houses they would be built
With stones and clay,
Or else just live in caves.

But God's almighty hands
Planted trees all over the land;
They are beautiful in their peace;
Wise in their silence.

They teach us, we must tend them.
They will stand long after we are dust.

&****&

Far Away

My Heart is searching the skies
Beyond the golden moon
Where thousands of stars appear
To be dancing in the snow
When the north winds blow,
Where the rising sun
Hides the darkness of the night
With tapestry across the sky.

My heart is searching the Heavens
Beyond the galaxies
Where warm south winds
Are waltzing on the fluffy clouds.

My heart is searching for you my love,
You are so far away
So every night I pray
And I wish that I could build
A stairway to the stars
To bring you back home again.

&****&

Narrow Streets

Nestled into an heavenly valley
A picture book village
Where the church tower clock ticks
Slowly chiming every hour,
Where simple life is savored
To the maximum.

Narrow cobblestone streets
Leading to the century old fountain
In the towns square
The old part of Rome,
You can hear the water whisper ancient stories
While splashing into the wishing well.

The streets winding through the town
Leading to scenic rolling green hills
Blanketed with vineyards
And lush pastures.

Surrounded by forest covered mountains
With the silhouette of medieval castles.
The narrow streets reach beyond
The crystal realms of ice
Where a million stars shine forth.

&****&

Silent Nature

I marvel nature's silent things
When the moon illuminates the night
And stars are shining bright,
When snowflakes gently tumbling down,
Yet, they never make a sound.

I gaze afar at the horizon
Where the ocean seems to meet the sky,
Where the sun is sinking into the ocean
Beaming a brilliant fire red and golden ball,
Yet, it never makes a sound.

Springs colorful landscape.
The summer's fruit bearing trees.
The autumn's picturesque splendor.
The winters bare fields.
Yet they never make a sound.

Turn man's hateful action into silent nature,
All wars would be silent then too!
Like lightning without thunder,
The world would be blessed
To never hear that sound.

&****&

Forever There

Beyond the span of years
With all the joy of love and tears,
There is a brightness that pervades
With multicolored shades!

Sometimes it's not enough
When life feels cold and rough
To hunger for direction
For happiness and perfection!

With each warm and gentle breeze
Patience shall bring peace
To the heart and soul
With faith you can reach your goal.

A journey into the endless twilight
Where the souls shall unite
But for the ones that cannot bear,
Trust in Him and He will be forever there.

&****&

A Time for Change

Outside my window a new day I see
There is a splendor in the morning
And only I can determine
What kind of day it will be.

It can be sunny or gray
Laughing and gay
Or bearing and cold
It cannot be bought or sold.

My own state of mind
Is the determining key,
For I am only the person
I let myself see.

I can be thoughtful
And help all I can
Or be selfish
Just think of myself.

I can enjoy what I do
Make it seem fun
Or gripe and complain
Get nothing done.

I can be patient with those
Who may not understand,
I know there can be beauty
In a desert with just rock and sand.

I can cope with faith and trust
Believe in what I say
But a change may be good
I intend to make the best of each day.

&*****&

Mother Nature

There is nothing anyone can do or say
I will always do it my way
If you don't give me respect
You will get hurt
On that you can bet.

Life is a mixture of sunshine and rain,
I know I'm loved and hated
And bring pleasure and pain,
I try to be good, as much as I can.

Sometimes I'm hard to predict
Very difficult to understand,
I can be very gentle and mild
But then, so very angry and wild.

None can ever convict me
And I will never pretend
Nor will I ever bend.
I'm here since the beginning
Long before man.

I'm Mother Nature
I rule over all the sea
The mountain and the land.
I'll be here forever
No matter how it all ends.

&****&

Alpine Meadow

Below the majestic mountain
A blanket of morning mist
Covers the hilltop meadow,
Reflecting the mountain shadow.

The sunrise lighting up
The morning splendor,
Slowly lifting up the misty blanket
Under the heavenly sky,
I sensed God was passing by.

The air is fresh and clean
The meadows look serene
The grass is lush and green.
Looking down into the valley
The Village church can be seen.

The shepherd, relaxing in the shade
Under a large pine tree,
His dog named queen
Watching the sheep
Feast on the lush green.

The beautiful sound of church bells
Fill the air
Echoing throughout the mountain
Valley everywhere.

&****&

Positive Attitude

Dream your own great dream,
Do small things in a grand way,
Take a light approach
To a serious matter,
Teamwork can be fun
It might cheer you on.

Catch an error before it happens,
Every job has some unpleasant duties,
Try to grin and bear them.
When the storms of life are raging,
It is good to help a friend
Knowing that the sun will shine again.

It is nice to work with friendly people
To be at one!
Bring joy into a heart
It only takes a moment
For a letter or a call
Delighting one and all.

Turn the page and take a look
Whatever the needs,
Lend a helping hand
Make every moment count,
Enjoy a perfect day
Think positive in every way.

&****&

Color's (#1)

Pale orange, rust foliage,
Yellow sun and sand,
Rich salmon pink,
Colors that never fade.

Deep calming colors
Inspired by a Greek landscape,
Oregano fields, olive trees.
The golden sun and pale stone
And a soft blue tone.

In pre Columbian time
Deep dark indigo,
A touch of ruby red,
Paler shades of gray and green
Earthly brown blended in.

Colors of life!
Dove white, fire red, raven black
Like Heaven, Hell, and death,
Virgin white,
The dream of every bride.

&****&

The Master's Touch

Under bright blue skies
A tropical paradise
Where palm trees line
The soft white sandy beaches
Surrounded by stunning azure sea.

Where temperamental majestic mountains
Reach up high to the heavens.
With endless waterfalls,
Lush orchards and beautiful
Flower gardens.

Where a thousand stars appear
The heaven is aglow.
Where the lovely golden moonlight
Caresses the surging tide
The islands magical beauty.

A dreamful lover's paradise
For young and old,
Joy ever abounds!
Every heart is welcome,
Here where memories abide

ALOHA!
&****&

Tick Tock

Life is like the clock
Tick- Tock
Second by second it ticks away,
Tick-Tock
Many times we can't wait
For the hours to pass,
So many times we wish
We could make it stop
that merciless clock,
Tick-Tock

Tick-Tock can't tell us
How long we'll be around,
But I can tell you this,
Enjoy your life!
Make every second count
As the time ticks away,
Tick-Tock,

Tick Tock! Tick Tock.

There Goes Another Day.

&****&

The Shield in My Life

It was a thunderous illuminating night
When he appeared and talked of the shield.
I was there, just a face in the crowd,
Elated by His energy and sight,
Enchanted by His charm and wit
As truth filled my ears
It eased my fears.

But then not by choice
He revealed the shield to me,
Invisible to my eyes
Hanging heavy from my chest
Like a storms eternity.

To my surprise he'd loosen the cord
That bound the battle shield.
I tried to stop it from tumbling down,
It crashed in front of my feet,
Shattering into many pieces.

My heart began to weep,
He smiled "Leave it and be free"
Sobbing deep moans rumbled through
My soul as I bent to pick up the pieces
And take them as my own.

I wrapped them in my shirt,
I will carry it a little longer;
I thought, without it I will be lost!
Walking to a hillside I laid the pieces down,
Leaving them buried on the hillside
I turned and walked away
With a flow of healing tears
Then hearing His voice within my soul
I felt free from all my fears.

&****&

Greener Grass

Rose Garden Lane is the name of the street
Where my new home is, my retreat!
It's far away from where I lived before,
Close to the Pacific Ocean shore.

Where palm trees line the streets,
Where the sun shines most of the year
And wherever you go
Different languages you hear.

The freeways are always jammed with cars,
Believe it or not, some nights
You can see the stars where movies are born
Where the earth shakes without being warned.

With beautiful beaches galore
And many miles of gorgeous ocean shore.
The home of Disney land where fun
Never ends till day is done.

Looking back I realize somehow
The grass looks a little greener now.

&****&

Blackout

I was a young boy back then.
It was a very scary time.
I was afraid of the dark
Wished I had my own flashlight,
Whenever the air raids
And total blackout began.

Total blackout became a strict law.
Whoever did not obey!
Was arrested and went to jail;
Might never see daylight again.

We had to cover all the windows,
Dim all the lights from shining bright.
No one would dare to expose
Even a glimmer of light
For the bombers to see at night.

Always sleeping with the cloth on
As the raids became more intense!
After the sound of the siren
We had no time to waste.

To the shelter we had to run
Praying and thanking God
For protecting and helping us
Make it through another day.

&****&

Equal Time

Only click here and not there!
But Dad, that's not fair.

You said you want to play games,
Well, you got one hour,
Next will be your brother James.

But Dad, I also like to chat!
Just play your games,
Leave it at that.

James has to write a school report
Your time is running short
So stop whining and messing around,
Your sister wants some time too
It is not all about you.

Dad, if I let James and Monica go first
Can I have more time?
No, for the rest of the evening
The computer will be mine.

But Dad, That's not Equal Time.

&****&

My Daily Bread

Love is my daily bread,
It alone gives life real sense.
Faith and trust is my daily bread,
They mean the most when
Walking down life's road.

Even through the time I weep,
There is still happiness in me
And so much to be thankful for,
As I have learned to follow him
Where all is peaceful and serene.

There is something that I do each day,
I give thanks for my daily bread,
Without it life wouldn't be quite the same,
I am thankful God blessed me that way.

In my early childhood, I lived,
Through many famish years,
Yet throughout my life I will always be
Thankful for my daily bread.

&****&

True Reflection

Mirror, Mirror on the wall
I know you're always truthful
But I wish you could show me all,
To view what will be ahead
Rather then leave me in the dark instead.

Every day I look at you
I can't believe that reflection is really true.
Well, I know you don't fool
But every morning
Must you be so cruel.

Where is the time
When you made me look so fine?
Now I should accept what I see
Because the older I get
The more painful it will be.

I like to see what the future will bring
When I'm called up,
Will I get my wings?
Now tell me Mirror, Mirror on the wall,
Is it true?
That seven years of bad luck will follow me,
After I smash you.

&****&

Schatzi

Miniature in size
But a beautiful bundle of joy,
A playful four-legged toy.

Many years ago
She was born on a farm
In a not very large barn
Among horses and cows
Where she lived in danger
Of being harmed.

It was love at first sight
We we're so glad that
We could save her hide.

She is very smart,
The best burglar alarm
With a heart!
She is as gentle as a lamb,
She loves to cuddle
And likes to go for a walk.
She is a good listener
It looks like she is trying to talk.

Life is short and we pray
That Schatzi our Wiener
Came into this world
for a long stay.

&****&

My Little Girl

Schatzi is her name,
She is miniature in size with a heart of gold.
For the last few days she was feeling very bad.
I got worried;
So, I took her to the vet,

When we got to the vet
She sensed that she was here before
Where she got an injection
And did not want anymore.

She sat down and refused
To walk through that door,
I had to pick her up and carry her in,
She started to whine losing her friendly grin.

The vet made some tests
He wrote out a prescription,
I had to trick Schatzi
Wrap the pills in pieces of ham
I thank God that my little girl
Is feeling herself again.

&****&

Gone to Heaven

It was in the evening when Schatzi began to moan,
She hardly could breathe could not walk on her own.
We quickly took her to the nearest pet emergency clinic.
She was in very grave condition, as soon as we got there
She immediately received oxygen care.
The prognosis was heart failure her lungs contained fluid.
Due to her old age her chances were not good.
I could not bear to see her suffer, I had to make
The most difficult decision in my life.

Tears were running down as I held her
For the last time in my arms.
Looking into her sad and tired eyes
they were saying I'm sorry
But I can't hang on any longer!
I cried, please don't go we all love you so,
Being deaf she couldn't hear me anymore,
But I knew she could feel my loving gentle touch
Which she loved so very much.
Seconds after the injection peace entered her heart,
She was blessed with sweet relief
But my heart was in pain with grief.

For sixteen years she was the most lovable, warmest loving, Gentle,
happy, playful, cuddlesome, beautiful, sweet little girl.
She will live in my heart for the rest of my life,
And I know I will hold my little girl again
When I meet her in Heaven.

&****&

Retired

Feeling of not being useful anymore.
Well, not young but still young at heart.
Not everything looks bright,
But I hope to add many more years of delight.

Now I have time for places to go and see
With maybe just you and me.
Be it rain or shine
I like to walk in the morning,
That makes me feel fine.

And I have time for things
I always wanted to do.
This is a new beginning not the end,
A blessing heaven sent.

Now when I look into the mirror
I do not like what I see,
He does not lie, it is really me.
That is what they call the golden years
I'm glad to still be here.

&****&

I Miss You

I am looking out the window watching the sun rise
From behind dark clouds I'm thinking out loud,
The question is why?

A sudden flash of lightning illuminates the sky,
I am sure I saw your shadow flashing by!
Then raindrops begin gently tapping on my window,
Like saying "let me in"

I am running out into the rain but you're not there,
With tear filled eyes I'm looking at the sky
Then out loud I cry, "I love you! I miss you!
Please dear God, tell me why?"

Comment
The Lord took my Mother in her best years of life.
She was very loving, I loved her very much.
What saddens me most
She never saw her
Grandchildren.

&****&

The Senior Years

No more worries of getting laid off
Or going on strike,
Now I can take as many naps as I like.
I have the time to start a new hobby,
Read many books, Travel around
And enjoy a senior discount.

I have more time now
For the to do honey list,
Things may take longer
I can do them at my own pace,
Only if I could find my tools
They're not in their usual place.

Now I can spend more time
With my Grandchildren.
I have many stories to tell
And time to listen to them well.

Looking into the mirror
I don't like my aged look,
Heaven may be closer but I'm happy
Counting my blessings, thanking God
That I'm still feeling good.

Now I realize time is a treasure
I appreciate every given day,
I have some time to volunteer
But this day is running short now
So I must stop right here.

&****&

I've Learned

To be more appreciative
As life is hurrying by.
I've learned what reality is
And also what is make believe.
I've learned to feed my soul, my mind
To leave my troubles behind.

I've learned to make everyday my best
Treasure each tomorrow.
I've learned that my heart filled with love
Is a blessing from Heaven above.

I've learned to cherish every moment,
Walk a straighter mile,
To give thanks for every morning
In such a short and fragile life.

I've learned it is not nice to swear,
A smile will get you almost everywhere.
I've learned for all the wrong I do
With faith I can get through.

&****&

I Am Safely Home My Dear

Do not stand at my grave and cry,
I am not here,
I do not sleep,
I am safely home in Heaven
For this once wondering sheep.

I am a thousand winds that blow.
I am the diamond sparkle in the snow.
I walk through the shady woods.
I fold my hands in prayer, and I know
I am the garden that lives within the soul.

Try to look beyond earth's shadows,
I sleep and dream upon cotton clouds.
I am the bright star that shines at night
I am the sunlight on ripened grain.
I am the gentle autumn rain.

When you awaken in the morning hush
I am the swift uplifting rush,
I am the quiet bird in flight,
I am now at peace forever.
I am safely home dear, I did not die.

&****&

Letters

Mr Woodbine
Park Drive
Gold Flake
CIGS

Words for every occasion
written down upon a page.
Words of love, sorrow, hope and hate,
For memories that never age.

A letter that can mean so much,
An ancient way to keep in touch,
Some will warm the coldest heart
Others may tear a life apart.

Living in a modem day of age
There are may ways to communicate,
Though it is nice to telephone,
A letter has a different tone.

It is not always a thrill
To hear the mailman ring,
Yet often I can hardly wait,
Hoping the mail won't come late.

$****&

A True Fan

Who admires you
In every way.
A special love
That will always stay.

To wait for hours
At your premier.
To take your pictures
Hoping that you will be there.

Always looking forward
To see you in your next play,
Fascinated with every
Character you portray.

Dreaming to be like you
In every way,
If only for one day.
A fan for life.

&****&

The Siren

I was only seven then,
When the first air raid alert began!
I was school ward bound,
I couldn't walk very fast
There was a lot of snow on the ground.

I never heard such a frightful sound before.
People started running in all directions
To the nearest shelter for protection.

I was scared and confused,
I didn't know what to do,
I wanted to get back home
But kids where running by me
Yelling "Come on!"
And it was closer to the school
So that's where I ran too.

After that frightful day
Life was never the same,
For five long years
The almost daily hair-raising air raid sirens
Did bring a lot of tragedy and fear.

&****&

The Worlds Best Medicine

Hugs are all natural and sweet
Without preservatives,
One hundred percent cholesterol free
And no prescription is needed.

Hugs are safe, in all kinds of weather
At any time of the day.
They are fully returnable
And make you feel much better.

Hugs are easy to care for,
Never need tune-ups or a battery,
A completely renewable resource
And they are maintenance free.

Hugs are not fattening
Never cause cavities.
They are very loveable
And are non-taxable.

Hugs have no language barrier,
It doesn't matter if you're rich or poor,
So don't wait until tomorrow
Hug someone today
You get one back right away.

&****&

ﺿ♣⚜♣ﺿ
Junk Mail

Free offers? Give me a brake!
Better read the fine lines
Before you order or sign
Or you will be spending
Many hours on the line.

It is almost a daily thing,
Where does it start?
And when will it end?
One could forever spend,
With so many "Free offers"
Chances to win,
They got you in a spin.

What about the beautiful trees
Being shredded
For so much annoying
"Junk mail" like this?

And all the email and spam,
Not the kind that comes in a can,
But the one on your PC
That never seems to leave.
Well, they say it is good
For the economy.

&****&

White Horse

The talk of death
Riding the white horse
I always thought
It was just nature taking its course.

Lancelot rode his mighty steed
His horse so white in his deed,
Lady Godiva her skin so light
The color transparent and oh so white.

What is this talk of death?
Of the white horse,
I always thought
It was just nature taking its course.

There is a cloud of pure cotton
Stranded high in the sky
Is this the white death
That is passing me by.

Purple haze, crystal craze,
So many brains in a daze.
So what is this talk of death?
I always thought
It was just nature taking its course.

Lawrence of Arabia had no remorse,
White was the color or his horse,
But mine is a different shade of the night,
My horse is known as china white.

&****&

The Moon Tears Legend

It happened a very long time ago
When a young chieftain
Won the heart of the moon.
Night after night
He would stand on top of the mountain
And sing to her
As she floated across the sky.

One night as he sang to her
The volcanic mountain did erupt
And she saw the young chieftain die
It made her very sad
She bitterly cried
Shedding golden moon dust tears
They fell sparkling crystal clear
To the ground.

For days heavy clouds covered the sky
You could not see the stars for many nights,
She was mourning and could not bring
Her Heart to shine bright.

Recited around the campfire
From generation to generation
For hundreds of years.

These semi precious stones
Almost looking diamond clear
The Indians named them "Moon Tears"
All around that volcanic mountain
The Moon Tears still can be found.

&****&

Mysterious Seven Seas

Wind, master of the waves
Rolling fast and high,
Ships sailing in the distant haze
Across the ocean far and wide.

Mountains deep of awesome height
Rivers join the ocean might,
Mysterious creatures inhabit the sea,
Icebergs floating open and carefree.

Hurricanes roaming wild and free,
Pirates dominated the seven seas.
A graveyard with many stories untold,
Oceans warm and cold.

Rugged seashores around the globe.
Beautiful beaches to behold,
Summers favorite place to be,
Around the mysterious seven seas.

&****&

Growing Up

Each day of youth was much to short,
The memories flash before me
I had blessings by the score.

My first serious kiss.
The blossoming love.
My first sexual encounter
When I reached the shore
My heart was beating like never before.

Love is like a happy puppy on strings,
Like butterflies gliding on magical wings,
Like the wind so wild and free.

My first solemn hangover
In a moment of despair
From the heartache I had to bear.

Yet while I'm growing within
I can plan and dream,
Love is all I want and need
To share in every way
Enjoy my life each day.

&****&

If Cars Could Talk

Imagine if cars could talk,
Many drivers would feel guilty
For the abuse and neglect,
Should be taught
About car care and respect.

If you treat your car
like you treat your friends
It will take you to the end.
Cars in a way have feelings too
Will perform better
When treated well.

As a car Doctor for many years
I know how they feel.
First I always listen to their heart,
To their squeaks and knocks
Before operating on
Their moving parts.

If cars could talk
A lot of trouble they would cause,
So many stories they could tell
About love joy, horror and fear
Some of the things
We rather wouldn't want to hear.

&****&

Always

Looking at our old photographs,
Remarkable you haven't changed,
You always have my heart racing.

I remember that day
We had that picture taken,
Vowing love forever.

Your love has me always
Endlessly spinning
Like a windmill
Dancing slowly in the wind.

Life would never be the same
Without your love,
You're always there for me,
A blessing from heaven.

&****&

Dreamer

Weaving riddles,
Unraveling clouded words
And the loose thoughts
Trapped in my desire
Like a wild fire.

I catch a vision I find love,
I see her come my way
I marvel at her splendor
She is more beautiful than a red rose.
Is she the one God has chosen?

I feel my heart hasten
As she comes closer,
I try to embrace her
But I can't move my arms,
A sudden breeze brushes my face
Before my eyes
My love is fading away.

The window had opened
A cold rush of wind
Interrupted my sleep
All I have is a dream to keep.

&****&

Color Your Life

Seize the moment and live for today,
Follow the yellow brick road
It might be the right way.

Take some time to think.
Believe in yourself.
Trust your dreams,
There is more to life
Than it may seem.

You get what you give.
Take the time to love and be loved
Before it all will be the past.
Every day and night
Try to thrust all your woes aside.

To unlock an empty day
Take some time to play
And make all the moments count,
Our days and years
Do swiftly mount.

&****&

My Soft Feathered Friends

The cold winter days have faded away.
The songbirds have come back
From their winter vacation and rest,
My garden becomes a special place
Where some will build their family nest.

I love to wake up in the morning
Hear their endless trill,
It is like a choir when angels sing.
I like to watch them in flight
Their beautiful colors they display,
It makes me wish I had wings.

I always make sure they have plenty to eat,
With a good variety of seeds.
The bluebirds like the peanuts best
They are picking them really fast.

I thank God for the birds,
I could watch them all day long,
It is also time to look out
For the cats that sneak around.

&*****&

Our Grandparents

They like kids, dogs, and cats;
Like to hold us in their lap
They like to take us to the park;
Are never in a great hurry,
Sometimes they do worry.

They tell all kinds of fascinating stories;
Give nice presents for our birthday,
They have some weird old toys to play;
Listen to what we have to say.
They understand us when we cry.
They don't always know the answers,
But they try.

They listen to funny music;
Have the nicest smelling house
And they seldom shout.
They can take their teeth out;
Know how to explain things
To Mom and Dad
Without getting mad.

They snore when they take a nap;
Always have ice cream and candy
In the house,
They have two cats,
And we have never seen a mouse.
They always buy what we're selling
For what it's worth; think we're the smartest,
Cutest kids on earth.

When they give us money,
They always say, save some for a rainy day.
Our Grandfather has a beard;
He doesn't like to shave

They are the only grown-ups who have time.
They always read us a bedtime story;
Then love to tuck us in and say good night.
Then they turn off the light

&****&

My Favorite Season

The summer has drifted away,
Nature is changing its clothes
The leaves turning red and gold,
What a beautiful sight to behold.

The festive days come into the scene
Most of the years harvest is in
With a bounty of wheat and corn
And I feel like new born.

A big fun day for the kids is Halloween
So many ghosts I have never seen
And the yummy Thanksgiving day
Is not far away.

The days are getting shorter
Winter will soon be knocking on the door
There is a gentle stillness,
That comes over the land.
I wish autumn would never end.

&****&

Mysterious Sky

First thing every morning
I peek at the sky
Looking friendly or not
I thank the Lord
For granting me another day;
For sending an angel
To protect me in every way.

This morning sky
Appeared in virgin blue
And the sun was smiling too,
By midday it darkened its complexion
With clouds in every direction.

The evening horizon appeared
Flaming red
And slowly fading to the west,
In the dark of the night
When the moon and the stars
Light up that mysterious sky
I often wonder where does it end
How far away is Heaven?

&****&

Morning Pleasure

The newness of each morning
When the sun begins to rise
What a blessed feeling
To be always in His sight
It brings a sense of peace
And no strife.

After a night long rain
To breathe the morning air
That is so fresh and clean
Like the soothing sound of
Falling water from a virgin spring.

Ah, and breakfast
The aroma of fresh brewed coffee,
Eggs, bacon and wheat toast.
The rush of work and play
Bring to mind another day.

All this morning pleasure
Love and laughter, dreams worthwhile
Are gone in a moment
As dark clouds move by.

&****&

The Fire Salamander Train

Moving at a leisurely speed
Steaming and puffing like a bull in heat,
Sixteen miles of rock-railway
Winding and unwinding
To the end of the line
Up five thousand feet
To the snow mountain alpine inn,
Serving a delicious cuisine.

A massive limestone mountain,
The highest in the lower Austrian Alps,
Over six thousand feet
With all year long snow covered peaks.
The alpine meadows are soft as down,
Mossy with many fragrant flowers
And coniferous forest.

You can hear the cowbells
Serene chiming sound
Echoing from the higher elevation,
Where the cows are grazing.
A panoramic view of the mountains
Around the incomparable colorful village
With the red rooftops in the valley below.

The maiden voyage of
The fire-salamander train
Began in eighteen ninety-seven;
Still climbing everyday
Up and down without any complaint.

&****&

A Winters Portrait

Natures falling snowflakes
Blanketing the prairie
Unforgiving cold winter winds
Reaching painfully into
Broken hearts.

The wolves are howling
As the clouds roll by
On that moonlit night.

The snow chilled hillsides shimmering
In the dazzling morning sunrise
Like the blazing stars
From above and beyond.

Throughout the winters round
The naked trees seem cold and dead
So silent all dressed in white,
An artists dream;
A stunning winter's portrait.

&****&

My Inspirations

To greet each day with a smile
Feel Gods love within.
To watch the sun rise
The world coming alive.

The golden days of my youth
With my Mothers warm and loving touch
My Dad who taught me so much
All their love to see me through.

To stand atop a mountain
Guided by God's hands
Feeling close to heaven,
Listen to the clouds symphonic sounds.

To live life to the fullest,
A journey around the world,
To places I have never been
When spring paints everything green.

A soft and warm blanket on my bed,
Apple butter thick and rich,
Saying grace before each meal
And someone to share it with.

&****&

Life's Gift

A heart that loves
Is sincere in many ways
A gift of God's creation
Patterned with grace.

A heart that knows
Love and happiness impart
Special words and kindly deeds
A helping hand in time of need.

A heart that is free
On the road we know as life
Takes what comes each day
No matter what the fate shall be.

A heart that laughs
Embraces all that's real,
A heart that stands proud
With thoughts that wander
Like a stream.

&****&

Another Year Older

The days of my youth are long behind,
My hair turned white
But my teeth are still intact;
My smile is ever so bright.

I've got corns on my feet
Well, I still can go dancing
And I like to walk brisk,
I have no hump or slipped disc.

I don't mind the few wrinkles.
My glands are still kicking ass.
I pee without assistance.
If I choose I can keep myself from passing gas.

I still have lots of friends,
Some may think I'm a total wreck.
To tell the truth,
Most mornings, I look like heck.

To tell you all my troubles
Would take way to long,
And when I tried I've,
Forgotten the gong.

I still have loads of fun,
My heart is with joy overrun,
So I have aged another year
But I'm happy to be still here.

OKAY... MAKE A WISH &
BLOW THEM OUT!

&****&

Strolling on the Beach

Strolling barefoot on the beach
On the warm summer sand,
Inhaling the fresh feathered sea breeze
And listen to the harmony from the waves,
As they roll in and out the sea.

Oh, the cool water feels so good on my feet,
It is a very pleasant place to be.
Watching children building a castle in the sand
And the bikini beauties bask in the sun,
Trying to get tanned revealing much at both ends.

The surfers seem to have fun chasing the waves
To ride them up and down.
Seagulls soaring through the air like kites on a windy day,
It is fun to watch them play.

What a gorgeous day of summer.
I didn't bring my bathing suit, what a bummer.

&****&

Fresh Fallen Snow

Fresh fallen snow
So pure and peaceful,
The trees all dressed in white
The snowflakes sparkle bright
Like the stars at night.

The dancing snowflakes
Swirl round and round.
Each crystal brushes the window pane
As they silently fall
Embracing the ground.

The patient moon hangs high
Peeking through the clouded sky,
Underfoot when all is still
You can hear the crunching of the snow
On the slippery street below.

Winter has arrived upon the scene,
Beyond the white and cold
The air is fresh and clean
It brightens each new day
Heaven is just a step away.

&****&

Computers

It comes in different sizes
At affordable prices,
It, may not always be understandable
But it's very dependable.

It uses a language by its own,
This has become worldwide known!
But it has a human problem too,
If it catches a virus
That will give it a screw.

And there is the mouse
Not the kind you might find
In your house,
If you move it around
It will not make a sound,
It gives commands
That only the computer understands,
Tap it gentle left or right
Click, click
It will bring another site.

The closest window to the world,
Oh, email you can receive and send
Without a postage stamp!
The most exciting feature yet
When you log on to the internet
You can chat with people all around
You can shop and browse
Without ever leaving your house.

&*****&

The Hills Are Alive

Thousand of years have formed
This natural paradise
Beneath the heavenly skies,
With high mountain peaks
And lush alpine pasture,
All formed by the Master.

Where generations have cared
For the city and villages around!
Where royalty once lived and ruled,
In ancient castles still standing proud.

In this historic city
Wolfgang Amadeus Mozart was born
On the XXVII of January MDCCLVI,
He died in MDCCXCI.
He was only thirty-five.
His music shall be forever alive.
In this undisturbed alpine landscape
The hills are alive
With waterfalls and lakes,
Where the movie,
"The Sound Of Music" was made.

A city of culture!
A pleasant atmosphere,
The Salzburger land,
Where nature got a helping hand.

&****&

Limitations

If you believe you can't do it
It will be so,
You should always try to complete it
Or let it go.

In the event of unusual circumstances
You delay
Use your best effort
All your determination will pay.

If you get another chance
You refuse to accept,
Don't complain
Your limitations will be a fact.

&****&

Treasured Time

Especially when I was a young boy,
I could hardly wait to hear the whistle blow;
The conductor's signal for the train to go.
As the train left the station
My older brother and I
Where waving to our parents goodbye.
It was an adventurous three-hour ride
Looking out the window
It seemed like the world was flying by.

We were on our way
To be with our grandparents in the country
For the summer to stay,
They loved having us around.
They were living on a small farm.
One summer we helped our grandfather
Build a new barn.

They had two oxen for pulling the plow,
A lot of chicken, rabbits and one
Jersey milk cow.

There were always a lot of things to do.
We'd go fishing to a nearby brook
Many times to the forest to pick berries;
To gather a lot of firewood.

Sometimes we found mushrooms
From which our grandmother made good soup.
She made the best flaky butter crust apple strudel,
She was the best cook.

The summers always went by much to fast.
We're thankful for all the time we could spend
With the most loving and best grandparents
In the world.

&****&

The Last Goodbye

When the phone rang at 2:30 A.M.
It was the call I did fear;
Didn't want to hear.
I rushed to the hospital
Hoping I was not too late,
My Mother had lapsed into a coma,
Her life was fading away.

The doctor told me, she might Not
Make it through the night.
Fighting cancer for almost a year,
Slowly, losing the fight!
She could no longer take the pain,
My Mother prayed,
Please dear God Take me away.

Still very young,
Always joyful and happy,
Enjoying life,
She was the best
Loving Mother and wife.

I sat by my Mothers side,
Holding her hand
She looked so peaceful;
Could not speak anymore!
I bitterly cried, "I love you"
I kissed her, it was my last goodbye.

Nearby I felt the presence of an angel
Waiting to take her to heaven!
The tears in my Mothers eyes
Were saying that she loved me,
It was my Mother's last goodbye.

&*****&

Love and Joy

Ho, Ho, Ho, Another year is about to go,
A new one is beginning soon
It may not come on a silver spoon,
Pray and enjoy each day
He may grant you a very long stay.

Let peace and joy fill every day
With friendship that lasts.
With love, a gift, enjoyed so much,
Trust all your heart and soul.
It will help you reach your goal.

For kinder thoughts and nobler deeds
Make each moment meaningful;
Extend a hand to those in need.
Love can make a world of a difference
At times when one needs a friend.

No matter what the season
Don't leave kind words unspoken,
Let Christ take you by the hand.
Inner peace will find its way
With love and joy on blessed
Christmas Day.

&****&

That's Amore

Thank you for mending
The unanswered years
Of many sorrows and tears,
With faith our love and desire
Will hold us together for life.

No diamonds or castle in the sky
Will ever replace our love and desire,
Together on Sunday
Under the dreamers apple tree
With buckets of delicious
Pink popsicles
Laughing and comforting each other
That's Amore.

I love to see you in
Your pretty crimson silk dress
You look like delicious strawberries
Like a beautiful innocent red rose
Without thorns waiting to be touched
That's Amore.

Noel

To Santa

"Noel", I'm not a child anymore,
I have no wishes for toys like before,
Now I wish and pray for Santa to bring peace
For the entire world to enjoy.

"Noel", for a night and day
No happier hours have come my way,
The lustrous glitter of the dressed pine
Each candle so colorful and bright
Like the stars at night.

"Noel", inside the house it is warm and cozy,
On the radio Christmas carols are playing,
Sitting close by the fire
Watching the dancing flames,
Mama would serve cookies
With hot cocoa and cider
On this blessed Holy Silent Night.

Noel", all the wonder that it brings,
A glow that brightens every heart
When the world comes alive
With joyful children laughing
At midnight the church bells ringing
With all the blessings God is giving.

&****&

Well, Winter

To all Winter lovers

All the leaves have fallen
The freezing winter swept in
Stripped my garden to the bones
Changed its makeup
Covered the landscape with snow.

The songbirds are gone
The stillness is like an illusion.
The winter brings its colors
It dresses all the trees in virgin white
Makes everything look so bright.

I do enjoy some of the winter things,
The sparkling :frost in the sun
The smell of wood smoke in the air,
A hot cup of tea with honey and rum,
Oh, and best, the time out from pulling weeds;
From cutting the grass almost every week.

Looking at things at a brighter side,
Soon winter will disappear
Spring will replace
The winter's messy snowy face
In the meantime
I just bundle up and count the days.

&****&

A Heavenly Dream

Did you know I dreamed
I saw us both in heaven!
The rules are different than on earth,
Everyone is welcome
They know you there.
Everyone is equal
You don't need an I.D

We were so young.
You in your white gown
With the angel wings
You looked like a queen.

Your baby blue eyes
Matched the heavenly sky,
With a red rose in your hair
To me you were the most beautiful
Angel there.

There, peace and joy did abound,
But we could not stay around
We still have to walk the road of life
Until the Lord decides.

&****&

A Sunny Christmas

It was Christmas day
Oh, not white like I wished for
Instead the sun was shinning bright
The wind was sitting still,
The only white I could see
Were cotton clouds above the hill.

For Santa, the clear and sunny weather
Must have been much better
To find all the houses faster
And bring all the presents on time.
Rudolf did save his batteries
To guide the sleigh
His nose didn't have to shine
At all that day.

The moral of the story is
Snow, rain or sunshine
I love Christmas every time
It is the birthday of our divine.

&****&

Baked Rabbit

I was a young boy then,
It was hard for me to understand
It always made me feel very sad
When one of the bunnies I watched
Growing up played with and fed
Ended up in the frying pan.

My Grandpa always tried to explain
He will not cause the bunny any pain.
I never liked to watch
When he held the bunny by his hind legs
And with his big hand
Judo chopped the bunnies' neck
Causing instant death.

These were very lean years,
A war was raging on
Everything was rationed
Once in awhile a baked rabbit
Was a welcome blessing!
Grandma's baked rabbits where the best.

Served with mashed potatoes,
Carrots and corn on the cob
With home baked bread.
Grandpa was a religious man.
He always said a prayer
Thanking the Lord
For blessing us with this food.

&****&

Love from A to Z

A miracle from God
B believe in each other
C character is developed
D demons are conquered
E every picture paints a memory

F faith is enlarged
G give unconditionally
H have faith when things go wrong
I inspiration is born!

J joy is planted
K keeps you close at heart
L live and love with Christian virtues
M meaning is found

N never judge
O offer support
P peace is embraced
Q quiets the fears

R remember the vows
S sunshine and rain
T to guide and strengthen
U understanding

V vision gives light
W wrongs are forgiven X exchange courtesies
Y yammering forbidden Z zaps you back to reality

&****&

Misguided Dreams

Drifting loosely in the wind
Misguided yet harvested dreams,
Sharing adventurous moments
On a journey into the endless twilight.

A yearning dream entered
And bowed silently
Embraced by desired love
And fantasies of naked dreams
Throughout the darkness of night.

The night giving way the to day
A change is taking place,
A sweet release from worldly care,
The pathway is made clear
From the misguided dreams.

&****&

A Magical Season

It may be cold outside
But the inside of my heart
Is warm with joy,
The magic of Christmas
Makes me feel like a little boy.

Mama is baking cookies
For the family and friends
To enjoy and share,
The Aroma is filling the house
Like the sky with cotton clouds.

There are many things to do,
Sending out cards to all my friends
Presents to be wrapped
Each a nice surprise!
It is time to decorate the tree,
Oh, and that frantic last minute
Shopping Spree.

Decorations are everywhere,
The flicker of candles;
Colorful decorated trees,
The store windows are nicely trimmed
With toys and beautiful things.

At Christmas time
I love to hear the Church bells chime.
A time for rejoicing
To celebrate with family and friends
My wish
Dear Santa, please bring peace
And don't let it end.

&****&

Embracing Life

Embracing life each given day
That lasts a lifetime through,
Clouds in symphonic play
That can never fade away.

To rise above each tide
When the pathway is made clear
To see what lies ahead
However long the years.

Whatever life may send
To set the spirit free
Through a looking glass for all
Around to see.

Love dear to the heart.
Lakes and rushing streams,
Fields with golden grain
The warmth of gentle rain

Faith that is stronger than fears
Dreams that may come true,
The taste of coffee surely helps
For all the things to do.

&****&

Grand Canyon

Screaming clouds race over
The majestic canyon into the night,
A canyon with splendor
Where nature is wearing a smile
As Douglas fir trees reach into the sky.

Pine trees have been standing guard
Over thousands of years,
Long before the dinosaurs roamed the earth
With no violence spared.

Much history lingers there.
Native people carved stories
Into the caves red stone walls,
If you listen closely you can
Hear them whisper in the wind.

Winter changes the landscape
Into a white wonderland,
A grand canyon,
More endurable than steel
Where all the illusions are real.

&****&

Coonhound

The freedom hill deep in
The Cumberland mountain range
In northern Alabama
A beautiful wilderness
Of native trees and wild flowers
Is the famous coonhound resting place,
The world's only coon dogs graveyard.

It came into being on Labor Day
September fourth nineteen thirty-seven.
That day two friends out deer hunting
With their famous coon dog named troop,
It was Troops last hunting day, he was fifteen,
When he was laid to rest there in the hills
Where he spend many enjoyable hours hunting.

Since then over 100 coon dogs
Have been buried at this site!
Epithets carved into many of the grave markers
With the affection and respect
For their canine friends!
Only true and tried coonhounds are allowed
To be buried in the unusual memorial park.

Each Labor Day there is a celebration in the park,
It offers the opportunity to pay
Tribute to man's best friend!
A barbeque picnic is held with entertainment,
Blue grass music, buck dancing, speech making,
Even a liars contest is enjoyed by hundreds of visitors.

At the site for the relieve and comfort
There are outhouses and lots of bushes,
But you must bring your own paper.
There are picnic tables and nearby is a fresh
Mountain spring with cold free stone water,
A place for all to see and enjoy nature at her best.

&****&

Life As A tree

I was a skinny four foot apple tree
With fragile limbs when they planted me.
Now I'm full grown over twenty feet tall
And this spring I'll be forty-two years old.

Every year I carry apples galore
That they always thank me for,
They take good care of me.
Every fall they prune my limbs
And feed me only the best things.

Birds did never build a nest
The neighborhood squirrels like me best
They crawl all over my limbs,
Nibble on my apples,
They become a real pest.

Every spring my apple blossoms
Are a beautiful sight
Pretty pink and white
I wear them with pride.

I can tell I'm getting old because
In some places I'm getting bald.
I don't know what my future is
Or how long I will be around
But as long as I'm fruitful
They won't cut me down.

&****&

Seeking For Answers

Would it be wrong,
To let more time pass
To provide peace of mind,
To let the perfect
Be the enemy of the good.

It is too easy to be detoured
In the daily hustle and bustle
While dwelling on earthly sod,
For all the precious moments
His gracious hands are evident.

In learning how to deal with life
There are many things I wish I knew
How to say the things I feel
For a day and a night and tomorrow
Without regrets or sorrow.

Walking down life's road
What is that you're whispering my friend?
Of all the beauty and answers
It is the Lord you are seeking

&****&

Let All the Church Bells Ring

Let all the church bells ring
Throughout the world
At midnight Christmas eve to celebrate
That holy night with joy and peace.

Let all the church bells ring
On that wondrous blessed night
Hear the angels sing,
Christ is born in Bethlehem.

Let all the church bells ring
Throughout Heavens
For all the blessings
The Lord does bring.
Let all the church bells ring at midnight
New Year's Eve for the new year to begin
With love and peace.

&****&

Life's Light

Stumbling in a world of darkness
Feeling my way through life
Never to see the sun set or rise.

Never to see my children
Nor the woman I love.
Never to see the guiding
Light from above.

Never to see
My Mama and Papa
My brothers and sister
Who always treat me nice.

Living in the darkness of the night!
I'm trying to find peace
In the things I understand.

I wonder what the moon
And the stars look like
Illuminating the heavenly
Sky at night.

I'm praying for a miracle.
It is hard to understand
What is my purpose in life?
Why was I born without,
The life's light.

&****&

Rhapsodies

I love the church bells ringing.
The crickets evening tunes,
The bursting rain clouds,
The ducks and geese flying south.

The stars sparkling like diamonds in the sky.
The old Roman roads between
The rolling green hills,
The autumn leaves rustling in the wind.

The thunders echo.
The wild honey on buttered toast,
The rolling waves dancing at the shore,
The first cry of a babe new born.

The mockingbird's morning song,
The whistling ships horn,
The first bus ride to school'
The joyful words "I DO!"

The words for love and peace;
The silent day when home is best;
The crimson sunset rhapsody,
The joy I feel within my soul.

&****&

The Brown Shirts

Over half a century ago
The peaceful time in Vienna
Turned into a hateful way,
When for some ethnic groups
It became too dangerous to stay.

I was only five then
When all the turmoil began,
Coming home from Sunday mass
My parents, my older sister, brother!
As I entered the apartment house
We heard gunshot noise ringing out.

When we got to the first floor
There was a group of men
In brown uniform
With a machine gun in the corridor
They were blasting away,
At a barricaded apartment door.

Two men stopped us and checked us out,
My Dad told them we lived on the third floor,
One of the Brown shirts yelled, "Go! Schnell!"
We were very scared and quickly ran up the stairs.

I didn't understand what was going on;
I asked my Dad, "What have they done?
Why are these men shooting into their apartment?"
My Dad tried to explain,
"They did nothing wrong,
They just believe and pray
In a different way"

The gunshots had silenced,
I heard the children cry
Calling for their Mama and Papa,
I knew them, we played together
They are my friends.

Looking out the window I saw these men
Taking the entire family away,
I expressed that I wished I were bigger
So I could help my friends,
My Dad said that if we tried to help them
These evil men would arrest and hurt us too.

My Mother was really scared
That the SA men, I call the Brown shirts
Wearing a red swastika armlet, would come back again
And arrest my dad
Because of the Jewish friends he had.

Every one became fair game
No one seemed safe anymore.
Many people were arrested;
Put into a concentration camp.

All because of the hate
And the persecution
Ordered By One
Tormented Mad Man.

Since then many things have changed
In this world of ours,
But too much prejudice still remains.
I never saw my friends again
But I will never forget them
Or that terrible, terrible day.

&****&

I Love Them All

They all have their charm
A lot of joy they bring
I do prefer some more than the others.
I love spring
The way everything bursts into bloom
Filling the air with sweet perfume.

I love summer, it means vacation time,
The forth of July and the awesome fireworks,
Picnics, swimming and outdoor fun,
The longer day light hours with the golden sun.

I love autumn's colorful display,
The cooler days it brings for a change,
Halloween's spooky day is always fun;
Thanksgiving feast is my favorite one.

I love winter neatly dressed in white
Like a beautiful bride,
But Christmas is the most
Joyful time of the year,
A peaceful silent and holy night.

Last the New Years Eve party time,
My resolution,
A healthy, peaceful year sublime.

Footsteps

Calling helplessly,
Somewhere in the night
Of darkness
I can hear
Very strange sounding
Footsteps
On the stairways.

And a trembling whispering
voice breathing slowly.

I can't make out what it is saying!

And then there is dead silence,
The footsteps and the whisper
Peacefully fade into the early
Morning light.

I'm left wondering
Will it come back?
Tonight.

&*****&

Three Wishes

Make Three Wishes

One day while strolling down the memory lane
I came across a tall huge colorful man,
He waved at me with a great big smile,
He said, "Hello, my name is Jinni, stay for awhile."

Very nice I said and I started to walk away,
He yelled, "Wait; Please stay, I got something to say,
I know a game, what do you say, will you play?
Won't you please sit down and stay?

He started to show me and really tried to explain.
I soon knew all about his game,
In his other life he was a free man,
All in all his life was a sham.

Then he asked me for my name,
And said this is how we do this play.
We both ask Aladdin, and then we will know
Who will stay and who will go.

If you win, you get to have three wishes,
Just say the magic word, and you're being pleased.
If you lose, then we trade places
I'll be free and you shall call the aces.

&****&

Love is Like

Love is like spring
When everything blossoms it is a beautiful thing.

Love is like climbing a mountain
When you reach the summit it is a great thrill.

Love is like ice cream
Once you taste it you can't get enough of it

Love is like playing the lottery
With the right combination you hit the jackpot

Love is like riding
On a roller coaster there are ups and downs.

Love is like taking a cruise
Once you're on board you hope for smooth sailing

Love is like a box
Of chocolate you never know what you get.

Love is like dancing
with the right partner then it will be heavenly.

&****&

The Beetle

Many were laughing and made fun
When the Volkswagen nicknamed beetle or bug
Made his first run.
Born during tumultuous years
He survived and is still here.

All over the globe
He became very popular and well known.
Whatever the weather
Rain or shine, hot or cold
Never let me down, he just went on.

He is not very big in size
But it was an affordable price
I'm trying to keep him alive.
He is a bit slow going over the hills
Yet very considerate on the gas bills.

With five Dollars of gas
He would take me very far,
He even became a big movie star.
For his size he has big rims
In the water he would swim.

He is an antique now
Forty years old, he may look tired
By no means has he retired,
Still looking better than any new style
He is good for many more miles.

&****&

A Light From Beyond

The midnight rain
Brushes against the windowpane
The day of grief embraces
The blessed peace
Through the darkest hours
Of the night.

The morning sky reaches down
Enjoying the light from beyond,
The magical rays from the sun
Promise a brighter day
Of hopes and dreams
Without clouds of dismay.

Faith is rays of light
A fulfillment of some deep
Longing for love and peace
Releasing thoughts of choices,
A well marked path
With a light from beyond.

&****&

Big Bang

How did it all begin?
Did Mother Nature have a bad day?
Pounding with all her force away.

Some scientist's say
There was a "BIG BANG"
Dark vapors covered the universe
Making a shapeless, chaotic mass,
That's how it all began.

The clergymen disagree, they say
God created Heaven and Earth
In six days
For all mankind to live in peace,
Declared it holy.

There is one thing that scientist's
And clergymen agree on
Zero hour is near and it is High time
For all men to restrain and agree
To prevent our world from ending
With a "BIG BANG"

&****&

All Within
(Abecedarian)

As the night drifts down and
Braves the storm,
Chimes of the church bells
Dance to the rhythm while the
Evening moon is reaching down,
Filling all hearts with calm.
Gentle rain is talking, all the
Hills turning green
In the twilight purple glow, the
Joyous month of June
Keeps all the colors in tune.
Looking into the clear blue sky
Mother nature happily smiles.
Northern stars shinning bright,
Outdoors heavenly light.
Poets heartfelt dream, a magic
Quill to write poetry for all world to read.
Reflecting hills dressed in white,
Splendorous sparkling diamond-like.
To feel the warmness of the rising sun
Unfolding life on earth forever
Valiant and vigorously from above
Within his blessed love.
Xenophiles plants
Yawn in boredom, life in the
Zoological garden goes on.

Transition

The frozen winter slopes
Slowly melting,
The shivering bare trees
Shaking their white covered branches.

It is the season
When earth wakes from the
Winter slumber,.
Spring trumpets skyward
Proclaiming sunshine.

Nature starts sprouting,
Bringing harmony and beauty
Of brilliant pastels
Into the garden we call life.

&****&

Dream Paradise

A star filled sky
Illuminating the beauty
Of the majestic
South island Tahiti beach
With a violet blue water lagoon.

Where sailor's dream of girls dancing to
The moon drenched hula hymns.

Where the warm Southern winds
Send God's love.

Where the stars capture the grandeur
Of the reefs with boundless love.

&****&

No Internet in Heaven

Young Eric coming home from school
All excited he is telling his mom,
"Today I've learned how to log on
And now I can email my dad in heaven,
Please mom give me his address."

"Well son, I'm sorry but that can't be done,
There is no internet in heaven."

"Just how do you know that mom?"
Asked her disappointed son!

"Our Pastor told me so, he said
Just say it all in your prayer
And you're Guardian Angel
Will take your message there."

"You see son,
Heaven is the place for peace,
Love and rest and thank God
For banning in Heaven
The internet"

&*****&

My Favorite Place

Sometimes I need to get away.
Just two hours north from the Golden Gate

There are a few small towns nestled
Around a large lake that nature made.

A beautiful place where fishing and boating is great!
Surrounded by mountains

That seems to touch the sky.
There is an awesome sleeping volcano near by.

Large orchards line the valleys growing grapes,
Fruits and nuts, and many other crops.

Rich with history, stories and legends.
There I find peace and renewed strength.

It will be my favorite place to the end.

&****&

GUIDING LIGHT

The open village church
Blessing all days and nights,
Its candles always burning bright.

With grace and peacefulness
The church bells calling me
To rise safely above each tide.

The open village church
Sharing Christian faith from the heart,
Healing all the wounds of yesterday.

The faith and joy in my heart
Is like the shining stars above
Overwhelmed with sparkling love.

The days with golden sunshine
Echo a song in the valley,
The beauty within the guiding light,
For He has given all we need.

&****&

Scarlet Sky

Beautiful sunset tapestry across the sky
Reaching down to me
Speaking of eternal love and peace,
Such happy feelings it brings.

In the scarlet sky angel voices
Singing His praise!
All the beauty here is on display,
Forever full of grace.

&*****&

Inner Vision

Larger than the past
A villain lost to love and truth,
He was tossed by raging waves,
Taken by the stormy sea.

Walking on a narrow road
With his arms hanging low
And his head bent down,
A skeleton from another time,
Drifting through the shadows
Searching for his love.

She could feel his presence
And hear him whisper in the wind,
"I have not forsaken you,
I only lived for thee my love."

Once a youthful loving pair,
Inside her heart she feels
His loving embrace,
Tears clouding her eyes
But not her memory of his love.

Looking at the sky,
In the clouds she could see
His image drifting towards heaven
To the light from beyond.

&****&

Christmas in Heaven

I listen to the angels sing;
To the Christmas choir up here,
For I'm celebrating Christmas
With Jesus this year.

Looking out the heavenly window
I can see the sadness in your heart,
My love, we're really not apart.

I'm not that far away.
I'll be your guardian angel from above
With all my undying love.

With my faith, a gift from the divine,
I believe that peace of mind
Forever we shall find.

Have a Merry Christmas sweetheart.
Please wipe away your tears
For I'm celebrating Christmas
With Jesus this year.

&****&

Precious Things

Your smile is like sparkling wine,
Straight from the sun blessed vine.

Whatever may come our way,
I shall love you more each day.

All the treasured gifts of love,
Heavenly blessings from above.

Where true love and hope abide,
Just look into your heart inside.

Friendship, all the joy it brings.
Many precious and special things.

Softly whispered summer rain,
Rays of sunshine shall remain.

Loving words and kindly deeds,
A blessed hand in time of need.

Mom's homemade vanilla ice cream,
Fishing with my dad at the stream.

Laughter and happiness sublime,
Strolling on the beach in summertime.

The sky lightens to a brighter blue,
The whole world comes into view.

&****&

My Birthday Wish

I make a wish;
Blowout the candles,
My family and friends cheer,
I'm thankful to be still here.

Every birthday I make a wish,
Some have come through
Others never do.

There are many things
I like to wish for,
Like love, peace, health and wealth,
To be able to fly,
Or Aladdin's magic lamp.

My candles are burning down,
Good health is what I'm wishing for,
Like the last words in the birthday song
"For many more"

&****&

Things of Joy and Beauty

New born babies crying,
Watching the golden sun rising.

My children's graduation day,
Giving the bride away.

To hear the church bells ringing,
Listen to a children's chorus singing.

Big band ballroom dancing,
Midnights moonlight romancing.

Sailing across the seven seas,
Full blooming cherry trees.

The glittering stars at night,
The majestic eagle in flight.

A rainbow embracing the sky,
Vanilla ice cream and apple pie.

Family and friends thanksgiving delight,
The wondrous Niagara Falls might.

The soothing sound of a fountain,
Climbing the highest mountain.

The treasured gift of love,
His blessings from above.

&****&

Aimless

My friends call me an aimless drifter,
I should settle down and get married
They all suggest.
I know it is a tough life as a drifter,
I'm always lucky to escape an arrest.

There are many trails and temptations
As a barter,
And I'm trying to amend.
I don't want to go through life as a martyr,
Often I pray for help
To defend.

I wonder what life will be here after,
Will I get any special request?
And no more tears, just laughter,
I do like to behest.

At one time I tried to be a broker.
I know how to graft,
But I'm just an aimless joker
For that I know my craft.

&****&

Splendor Moments

Snow is falling gentle in motion,
Winters virgin white gown,
January, sparkling time,
February, Valentine.

While north winds waltzing
Over the hills,
It feels so nice by the fireplace
Roasting marshmallows.

Children building a snowman,
Riding on sleighs,
Rolling in the snow,
Laughing having a good time.

Walking in the snow
while the sun is hanging around
Caressing the snowflakes
Splendor moments!
This is a day the Lord has made.

&****&

To Be or Not

Will there be a beyond
After this century?
Let's pray that men will overcome
Their stupidity.

Wisdom is the tree of life,
It is more valuable
Than any treasure on earth,
So why do men always argue
And never agree?
They are not deaf or blind,
Do they just simply refuse,
To listen and see.

Soon it might be too late.
It is high time for the world
To realize that we're all dancing
On very thin ice.

The United Nations should demand
That every war should be conducted
Like the Olympic events,
Just competing
Not to devastate each other
To the end.

&****&

Edelweiss
(Nonet)

Edelweiss with white and woolly leaves,
Small flowering plant of the alps.
Native to the high mountains
Of Europe and Asia!
Beautiful and proud,
Preciously rare,
For ever
It shall
Live.

&****&

Far Beyond

A hidden splendor
Far beyond the horizon
Like in heavenly paradise!
The fences are painted white,
All the sheep grazing inside.

There is no winter time,
Every day starts with golden sunshine.
The clouds are rosy pink
Like the angel wings.

There is a precious calmness,
A loveliness that pervades
Around the mirrored wild
Flower meadows.

Where the beauty of nature
never hides
Love and devotion abide.

&****&

Colors #2

A rainbow's arc
Vermilion red, lemon yellow,
Light green, virgin blue,
Colors that speak to you.

Summer splendor,
Dogwood blooms in ruffled white,
Velvet roses, golden sun glow,
Colors of pure delight.

Autumn colors foliage,
Rustic brown, crimson red,
Orange, green shimmering gold
All for the eyes to behold.

Mozart's magic flute
Resonates with brilliance of colors,
Most ethereal violet
To bolder violet hues.

Flaming sunset against the pale blue sea,
Green hills and sparkling streams,
Waving fields of goldenrod
Nature's colors that display a lot.

&*****&

My Photo Album

From the beginning to the end memories
Of years delight,
Pictures that tell stories in color
And in black and white.

It has been a long journey
From the first picture
My mom and dad took of me,
Some brought tears
Others happy smiles,
My priceless treasure for life.

Sometimes I wish I could go back
To see my mom and dad again,
My grandparents and friends,
Go to the many places we have been
And to all the joyful things
We have done and seen.

All the sad and happy times
We went through,
The birthdays and Christmas's too.
No artist could paint more beautiful picture
That is so full with grandeur
As the pictures in my photo album.

&****&

Flashbacks

Great memories of the best times
And the worst of times
Of the younger years!
It was the age of wisdom
The age of craziness,
Days of laughter, days of tears
Nights of joy and fear.

Simple pleasures seemed more valuable.
It was the spring of hope,
The winter of despair,
I had everything before me
But I had nothing to share.

I had a different perspective,
It was a season of sunshine;
A period of darkness!
Was I going directly to Heaven
Or straight the other way.

A time to flashback, to pause,
To look about and beyond
My garden gate
Into this challenging world!
When faced with life's test
I'll be content
Knowing that I have tried
To do my very best.

&****&

WINDOW OF TOMORROW

Window of tomorrow's changing world,
It shall be like the coming of dawn,and
Nature promises a rhapsody.
Do believe in prayer without any doubt,
One day the view will be clear for all the see
When the sun is peeping through the clouds.

Open all the windows
For it makes one wonder,

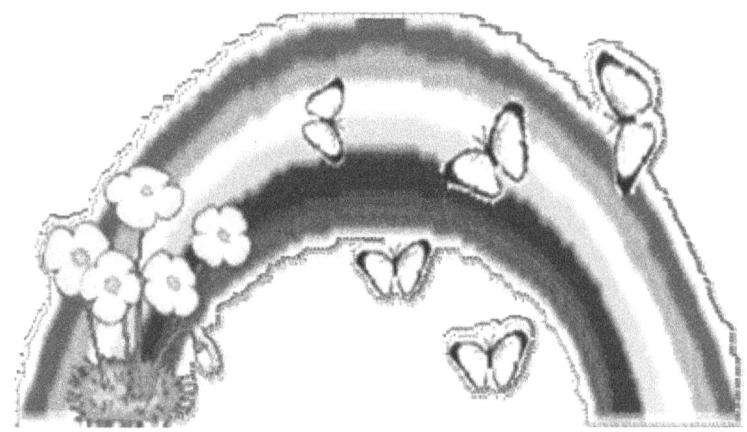

The beautiful colors it brings,
Oh, so rainbow like
Making the sky so bright
Of happiness and peace.
Raise your eyes towards heaven, it is
Reflecting in many ways,
On Lord we can depend,
Windows of tomorrow's world.

&****&

Book price $16.95

&****&

www.ingramcontent.com/pod-product-compliance
Lightning Source LLC
Chambersburg PA
CBHW021012090426
42738CB00007B/761